The Silent Patient

—— A TRUE STORY ——

D1003001

DARLENE JAMISON

Nurse, Writer, Fund-raiser, Volunteer Nurse, and Artist

PAGE PUBLISHING, INC.
New York, NY

First originally published by Page Publishing, Inc. 2017

ISBN 978-1-64082-603-8 (Paperback)
ISBN 978-1-64082-604-5 (Digital)

Printed in the United States of America

Acknowledgments

Primary thanks goes to friends, family, and people that I have met throughout my life. Most importantly, to Jesus Christ who led me and directed my steps. He gave me the knowledge to write this book and be able to live and tell about it. Because without Him, nothing is possible, and with Him, everything is possible. I was blessed to have a special man in my life after my last divorce; he encourages me and loves me for who I am, and I'm thankful for that. Special thanks to Jim Cox of KEZK 102.5 FM radio station. Mr. Cox helped me, with the kindness of his heart, with my first self-published book. This particular poem is dedicated to Mr. Jim Cox.

He is a man with integrity,
Fairness, and good insight.
Honesty is seen in his eyes.
There was a glow that was bright.
He helps others and helped me as well.
Just when I became discouraged, Jim cleared my trail.
I had walked this trail for many months,
Working to see my dream come true.
Just when I was about to give up,
God sent you.
We must never give up on anything in life.
We must be diligent and don't give up the fight.
God will send someone that will show us the light.
Thank you, Mr. Cox.

Wall of Tolerance

The undersigned co-chairs of the

National Campaign for Tolerance

do hereby authorize that the name of

Ms. Darlene Jamison

be placed on the Wall of Tolerance

honoring those who are taking a personal, public
stand against hate, injustice and intolerance, and
who are leading the way toward a more just
America as Founding Members of the National
Campaign for Tolerance

Authorized this 5th day of July 2004.

MORRIS DEES
CO-CHAIR

ROSA PARKS
CO-CHAIR

e Life at a Time

rness of breath, anxiety, nau-
ation. Because Aunt Margaret
., the nurse obtained oxygen
ing weekend, she obtained a
plications. Eventually, those
peaking with the doctor and
st, she was able to obtain
the work of breathing.

ng abnormal, she was in touch
to time solving problems
ciplinary approach to care, she
numbers, if necessary. For
social worker, so between the
the family with coping skills.
___ results, and because
with her visits, ___
holistic and supportive care
mily unit"). With the hospice
uld be a family member, not
a nurse. This lifted a weight
be a niece, a cousin, not an

advice and counseling. "I'll
uate from college." My aunt
et goals; she and my uncle
tirement, so my uncle needed
needed to hire caregivers to
worker was able to help them.
occupied bed; but what about
hile reporting to the RN, the
ins how to check for and pre-
many other tips on care of a
nia provided ministry to Aunt
arranged for communion. On
neral services after death, and
and bereavement follow-up.
ped without our volunteer Gail
onto food, managed her store
ded reassurance; or gave her
ld run errands, go to church or
also told me of one volunteer
sation for a hospice patient's
his wife in the nursing home,
physician with experience in
ogist. The nurse had another
macist. There was also an on-
hours' questions or c___

To A Director of Nursing
The following poem was submitted by Darlene Harrison, LPN, O'Fallon, MO

I met her about ten years ago,
our paths crossed again by fate.
She rushed onto the elevator,
to avoid being late.

After ten years she hadn't aged at all.
Her outstanding demeanor still glowed.
A professional and intelligent nurse,
reaping the good that she had sowed.

I smiled at her and thanked her,
for all the encouragement she had given me.
The seed that she had planted,
had sprouted limbs from the tree.

She was now Director of Nursing
and if was her first day.
I was happy to know we had a leader,
that would work with us in every way.

I told her that I was now a licensed nurse.
She had inspired me and others years ago.
Her supervision was like no other nurse.
She taught us what we needed to know.

She was always teaching and helping others.
These qualities are a must in our field.
A beautiful person with a heart of gold
from her we learned to build.

To this day she doesn't know,
how many people she helped along the way.
She never slighted anyone,
I sincerely thank her to this day.

It is a must to treat everyone with respect.
Because you never know whose path
you may cross from the past.
Always keep in mind that your first impression,
might also be your last.

Once again thank you for sharing your stories with us
and thanks for making a difference!

To the Readers

My mother was a single parent who kept a tight rein on her children. Every night, when I was a little girl, my mom would make me sit down and read the Bible to me. Sometimes, I would read to her as I grew. My family was very poor, but she always managed to keep something on the table for us to eat. When I turned eleven years old, I would hang around the kitchen to learn how to cook. On most of the holidays, we would have a feast on the table. She was an excellent cook. We all were grateful for those holiday meals. When I turned twelve years old, my mom allowed me to cook meals for the entire family. This was enjoyable to me because I loved to cook. Even to this day, I still do enjoy cooking. When we had extra food, my mom would have me deliver meals to some of the neighbors that didn't have enough food to eat. So, I guess, my volunteer work began back then even though I didn't realize it. God was preparing me to do much more of His works in the future. My mother and I had a stormy relationship when I was in my teens and young adult years. I realize now that she was not perfect, as no one is, and she did the best she could.

In the last year of my mother's life, we became best friends. We spent a lot of time together when I had a family of my own. She enjoyed spending time over at my house every week. I taught her how to fish and drive a little bit. She was so proud of herself, it was written all over her face, which made me happy too. We confided in each other and learned a lot about each other. Sometimes, she would have tears in her eyes saying, "I never thought I would have so much fun and go places that I've never been before." I would look at her and say, "Don't cry. It's a pleasure to see your eyes light up with joy."

Little did I know that it would be the last year I would see her again. She died that year at a young age of sixty-four years old. I have one daughter and one son and grandchildren now. My mother knew and loved my children, but she never got a chance to see my future grandchildren. I'm sure they would have brought her much joy as they do for me. My mom never liked to have her picture taken, but I would always sneak a few pictures every now and then. The only picture she willingly posed for is when she was saluting military style at the World War II museum. I used that picture for her obituary. It seemed appropriate since she passed away on Veteran's Day.

I worked as a nurse for many years for various long-term care nursing home facilities. Later, I decided to open an art gallery but closed it after taking a tremendous financial loss. But I never gave up my love for art or writing. So I started donating art paintings to different charitable organizations to raise money for people in need.

At some facilities where I worked as a nurse, some of the employees did not like me, and they made it well-known. That didn't bother me as long as I was doing the right thing. The main reason why there was a group of staff members who didn't like me was because I pushed for professionalism and customer service for the patients, one another, visitors, and family members. I know God had me work at various long-term care facilities to spread love and to teach others the importance of these things. I did the best I could, and most importantly, I did what God wanted me to do.

I have learned a lot over the years, and now I realize that Jesus was preparing me to do certain things in life ever since I was a child. Everything happens for a reason in life. It may be good or it may be bad, and it may also condition us to do certain works and master them through Jesus Christ. No school can teach this. When God chooses us to be one of His students, this is something that no one can ever take away from us except the One who has given it to us. You've heard that practice makes perfect, and this is true. To master something, we must continue to work at it. It is also very important to absorb knowledge and learn all that we can. Any knowledge gained is beneficial not only for yourself but for others as well.

As life unfolds itself to us, always do the best that we can. Most importantly, always make time for God and teach your earthly family about Him. Start your children out early about Him and they too will believe, and this will help guide them in a good direction in life and choices we must make in life.

To understand life, you must see it through your heart. To feel life, you must live life to its fullest. To grasp at life, you must strive for contentment. Contentment is only met through the Grace of God. Everything He does He does for a reason. You may not see the reason things happen, but eventually, when the time is right, He will let you know. Not only is it good to encourage others, sometimes, we also have to encourage ourselves too. Through my eyes and heart and through the eyes and heart of others, I paint and write what I see and feel. Thank you for purchasing this book. I hope it strengthens you, encourages you, and makes you see things as they are to be seen in life.

I was born on July 10, 1957. My childhood was that of a poor life, but somehow, my mother managed to keep all of us fed even if it was just flour mixed with water and fried. It made our stomachs full, and on some occasions, we would have meat and side dish. I remember that well 'cause I was the youngest in the household of six. My mother had nine children all together, but the other three were not living with us. That's a whole story in itself. When I was six years old, my mother couldn't afford to purchase shoes for some of us. One day, on my way to school, I had on a pair of shoes that was two sizes too large for me, but that was all I had to wear, so I stuffed tissue in my shoes at the toe parts, like my sister showed me how to do it to make the shoes stay on my feet. Well, on the way to school, one of my shoes slid off my foot and I tried to catch it, but it was too late. It slid down into the sewer. All the kids laughed at me, and I was so ashamed and started crying. One little girl in my classroom said to come go home with her and she'll give me a pair of her shoes. So we walked to her house (I was only wearing one shoe and held the other shoe in my hand). Upon arriving at her house, I tried on multiple pair of shoes, and none fit 'cause they were too small.

My friend suggested that we not go to school 'cause the kids would still be laughing at me, and we decided to watch cartoons, and we fell asleep. When I woke up, it was a whole hour past the time I was supposed to be home from school. I woke up my friend and rushed home wearing on socks on my feet 'cause I couldn't walk in only one shoe. But I was afraid to leave or throw the other shoe away. I frankly did not know what to do but to hurry home and explain why I was late and didn't go to school. By the time I arrived home, I saw my mother crying and talking to the police. She screamed, "There she is!" I knew I was going to be in trouble, but surely, for a six-year-old, I thought she would understand my child rationale as to what happened to me. I got a whippin', and she wasn't concerned about how I couldn't go to school with no shoes, so I thought. She must have listened though 'cause, in a couple of days, a lady picked me and my sister up and bought us some boy-looking shoes, and this was in the 1960s.

My sister and I was ridiculed by the other kids at school, but we had no choice but to take it 'cause, at least, they fit and our feet wasn't hurting in them. Eventually, we got some uniform shoes. Oh, I didn't say that we all went to parochial schools, did I? Mom worked her fingers to the bones—scrubbing, cleaning, and ironing for the church and the school every day—to pay for our education. She said, "I don't want you girls going to public schools. I want you all to be smart and act the way God wants you to act." There were things I just didn't understand as a child, and being the youngest wasn't easy in the household. When I turned fourteen years old, I had to attend public school 'cause my mom couldn't work anymore at the churches or schools for me, the last one to grow up. So I had to attend public schools, which became a real serious problem. It was entirely different from parochial schools that I was used to. Some of the black school students bullied me and called me names every single day.

One day, one of the girls told me that seven of them were going to jump on me coming Friday, so be ready to get beat up. It was Monday, and I was scared. I told my mother what was going to happen to me on Friday. She told me that she couldn't do anything but give me advice. The advice was that you find out who the ringleader is and, when I find out, no matter what or who is hitting me, to take the ringleader out and punch as hard as I could. Then she said that once the ringleader falls, the followers will bail out 'cause they'll be afraid.

When Thursday came, they taunted me and called me names all the way home. No one helped or even tried to stop it. They just followed 'cause they were cowards. I have no respect for cowards even till this day. I was so scared I barely slept that night 'cause Friday was the next day, and I probably was going to be killed or severely injured. Friday morning when the bus arrived, I got on the bus and the girls immediately started calling me white girl, I think I'm smart and cute, and how they were going to pulverize me this evening. I had to go to school 'cause, if I didn't, they would think I was a coward, and it would just get worse for me. The male teacher heard about it and tried to correct the girls in the classroom. Then they just said that the teacher must be my boyfriend, and they started talking about that for the rest of the day. The school bell rang for us to leave school and get on the bus to go home. I was really scared by now, but it was do or die, and I was going to die trying to defend myself.

When I got off the bus to go home, I had to walk a few blocks before I arrived home. I turned around and looked and thought, *Oh my god.* There were hundreds of kids behind me yelling, "Fight, fight, fight." I clutched my schoolbooks in my arms and continued to walk home. But one girl was cursing me and calling me names and saying, "You're not in Catholic school now, bitch. You're with us, and we're going to kick your ass!" That girl was the ringleader. While I was walking, this coward punched me on my back as hard as she could, and I immediately became angry. I dropped my schoolbooks and looked into her face like Mike Tyson, the fighter. She fell backward like a tree and was unconscious. I stood over her, waiting for her to get up so I could throw her a flurry of fists again, but she was out. Her buddies stood there and didn't attempt to fight me. Everyone just started laughing at the girl on the ground. I picked up my books and quietly went home. When Monday came, the girl that I knocked out did not show up for school for a few days. I was happy 'cause she was nothing but evil trouble.

At the age of fourteen, my mom allowed me to go to work. I was tired of being hungry and not having clothes or shoes to wear. I got my first job at fourteen at a popular St. Louis restaurant (I told them that I was sixteen years old). My title was the salad girl. I served soup and salads to the customers at downtown St. Louis. My mother wanted me to buy groceries and give my check to her, and I agreed to buy food, but I was not going to give my whole check to everyone living in the house that was older than me. I felt it was not my responsibility to take care of adult people when I was the youngest, and I'm the one who should be taken cared of. This really angered my mom. Her response was that she took care of me and so I should give my check over. Although I know she did the best she could, I was not going to do that. I felt that if I could work, then my other siblings who were in the household at that time should work too, and if they did work, they wouldn't have to fork over their whole check.

At the age of sixteen, I acquired a job at a well-known insurance company known worldwide. I had told them I was eighteen years old in order to get that particular office job. A couple of siblings asked me how I got a job like that so they could go apply. I was also asked what should they wear and other things for an interview. I told them information that only God could have put in me. Also told them who I was and where I worked at in the insurance company. They followed my instructions and were also able to land a job for themselves there as well. There was a lot of lying and jealousy against me by some of my siblings, and of course, my mom believed some of them. Sometimes, my mom would not listen to me when I told her that there were things that were not true.

I came home, one day, from work and discovered that my mother had moved out and left me alone at the age of seventeen. So I had to figure out how to fend for myself. I was hurt because, the week before, my sister told me that they were moving out and was going to leave me all alone and I would not know where they were moving to. It turned out to be true. My own mother didn't give me the address 'cause she was angry about me not giving up my entire check to her. Also, my mom had a boyfriend that I didn't like, and he didn't like me either. I could tell by the way he would look at me with dislike. That's 'cause I saw through him. I believe he also had an influence on leaving me at the apartment alone. It was like it's either me or your daughter. So she chose him and other siblings over me. It hurt, but I didn't show it to her. I just continued to work and find a cheaper and smaller apartment to live. I had to grow up fast. It was sink or swim, but something inside me would not allow me to sink. It just made me mentally stronger as I learned to grow up.

I met an eighteen-year-old man whom I fell in love with and got pregnant. I knew nothing about birth control or all the other girls in the family knew about, but I was never taught about a lot of things. It seemed as if my mother was tired of all the children she had to deal with her entire life, and since I was very independent, I guess when she said you're stronger than the rest of the girls, you'll be okay. That statement didn't sit with me well either. But I made sure I didn't cry or show emotions like she probably expected me to do when she returned a week later, asking me for twenty dollars. I had money in my pocket but wasn't going to give her a dime of it. I told her to ask the sisters she took with her for money, not me, 'cause I don't have anything for her. I thought, *The nerve of her leaving me alone, then asking me for money so she could take home—wherever home was—funds for her family. Why doesn't she ask her boyfriend for money?*

My firstborn baby was a beautiful baby girl. Her father denied her till she reached her thirties. When my daughter became old enough to ask me who her real father was, I told her his entire name. She wanted to see him when she was seven, and he came and stayed a brief time. After my daughter was born a year and half later, I had my second baby, who was a beautiful baby boy. My son's father and I got married. But his father, Jim, wanted every woman he saw and started sleeping around with them. His father and I got divorced, and he went on to marry someone that was way younger than I was.

That's life. You never know which way it will go or land. My second marriage was to a man whom I will call Ollie. We stayed married for almost fifteen years, but in the last two years of my marriage, we slept in different rooms 'cause I chose to. He also cheated on me, and I didn't want him to touch me anymore. Now that my children were in their teens, I went and got my GED and took college classes as a CMT (certified medicine technician) 'cause, prior to that, I was a CNA (certified nurse assistant). I didn't stop there, so I went to nursing school and became an LPN (licensed practical nurse). By then, the children were adults. My daughter had gotten married, and my son graduated from high school. You see, my children were the most important people in my life, and I made sure they had the best childhood I could give since I didn't have one. I made sure they had all the things that I never had growing up, especially rules, expectations, love, education, and so many other things that any good parent would do for their children. They were my life, and they have children of their own now, and I love them just as much. I smile thinking about my extended family. Both of my children are wonderful parents, and I am proud of them for that and happy that Jesus gave me those two children of mine. I was very protective over my children and grandchildren.

After a couple of years of being a nurse, I wrote two self-published poetry books, opened an art gallery, did fund-raisers for people in need, and volunteered as a nurse during any disaster. You don't have to have money to volunteer to help others. Just use your God-given gifts and knowledge, and all will fall into place. I had my first live radio interview about my first poetry book by one of the general managers at KEZK 102.5 FM radio station. Rosa Parks mailed me a Wall of Tolerance Certificate to be placed on the Wall of Tolerance. North County in St. Louis did a front-page article of my art gallery. So much was happening so fast, and I had the will and energy to keep up with it.

Laziness and quitting was not in my life 'cause I would not allow it. All nurses get a nursing newspaper article of one of my poems called "To a Director of Nursing in 2003." You will see some of my achievements in this book in hopes of encouraging others to never give up. Most of the time, as a child, I didn't have a bed to sleep on, only the floor. I want people to know that if I can continue and bring myself up from the ground, then they can too. It can only be done with faith, love, hope, and determination through Jesus, who watches over us all in life. Life is what we make it, and life doesn't have to be what someone else chooses for you 'cause you will have to make the ultimate decision and be adamant with your steps in life.

As a black woman, it was hard finding truthful directions on publishing my books and many other things in life. A friend of mine named RN coworker, was passing by the nurse's station one day and overheard my conversation. He simply said, "You're an artist and writer. Just self-publish it yourself." So with that instant wisdom, I listened and that's what I did. So you see, it pays to listen 'cause it may be a message meant for you to hear in life. We are still friends till this day. Friends are hard to find, so when you find one, hold on to that friend 'cause there are a lot of deceitful people in the world. One has to be able to distinguish that within themselves. Your first instinct is normally correct if you ask God for wisdom or anything He will give it to you as long as you are using it for the good. I love to write, and whenever I write, I try to encourage, help, inspire, and educate others. So this book is for you. Let things show that no matter the color of your skin, education, background, or strifes, you can always overcome things in life and learn to move on for a better you.

I worked for various LTC (long-term care) facilities. It was a day-to-day battle getting the staff in dietary, housekeeping, and others to carry and produce excellent professionalism, care, and respect and stay focused on our duties. Abuse does exist in LTCs and hospitals. I know 'cause I was an inpatient in a hospital without a voice and fired many health care workers in LTCs, so I can speak from firsthand experience on these subjects. After being a nurse for about a year or two, I had many promotions (that I didn't ask for) as an administration assistant, assistant director of nursing, case care management nurse, supervisor positions, charge nurse position, conducting in services on a regular basis. So I have worked from the bottom as a CNA all the way to being a CMT, then all the way to being a nurse.

I figured years ago, how can I be a nurse when I don't know all the steps in supervising others the correct and proper way to do their job as a charge nurse? It will probably be hard for you to read the stories I am about to write about our health care. Not all health providers do a poor job, just some of them. I guess I could say at least 75 percent of them. Very high percentage, huh? Yes, it is too high. It was my job to make a difference. Even if I just reached one or many, it was worth it. At least they would know how to care for our patients or residents. Also, they would know how to show excellent customer service to patients, one another, visitors, family members, and those outside the workplace as well.

At one LTC, a resident had told me that some of the patients were being taken outside for a scary joyride downhill outside for laughs, and the patients were scared and screaming as they were being toyed with. The resident told me that the charge nurse on staff at that time when I wasn't there did nothing about it, and he waited for me to come to work the next day to tell me 'cause he knew I do not tolerate this sort of behavior. All staff that participated in this were fired including the charge nurse. I was deemed as a too-strict nurse, and names were made up about me by the staff. I didn't care about that. What I did care about was doing the right thing. After all, when it is time for me to expire in life, I don't want God to turn away from me when I had the power to do what was right. Remember this: we all have to answer as to what we do on earth. Sometimes, we pay on earth and afterlife. Here is a poem I would like for you to read. The name is "Weather the Storm." I wrote this poem over a decade ago.

Weather the Storm

Stand tall, firm, and steady,
Just like the tree in a storm.
The branches sway this way and that way,
But it stands without harm.
Plant your roots on good and solid ground,
Just like the tree and steady you'll be.

After the storm, you hear only one sound.
The birds singing joyously
And a rainbow that's colorful and free.
The sun shining so bright
Lasting all the way till night.

Stand tall like the tree.
Let your light shine bright.
When you weather the storm,
You'll have better insight.

When the wind blows strong,
Bend and don't break.
Do goodwill for all
And God will never let you fall.
Sunshine always follows the storm.
Storms come and storms go.
Learn to weather them,
And beyond you'll see the glow.

Plant your roots on good soil
So when the storm does approach,
The roots won't wash away.
It just gets stronger every day.

God's blessings are abundant.
His grace is everlasting.
We thank you, dear Lord, for staying with us.
In your name, we rejoice and sing.

I wrote this poem many years ago 'cause we all face storms in our lives one way or the other. I, as so many others, would like to see peace among our fellow men and women. Speaking of peace, let's go to another conduct matter in an LTC facility number 2.

I was sitting behind the nurses' station doing some charting when a CNA got in the face of a patient by the nurses' station and was yelling at him for reporting the staff. I had to demand two to three times for the staff member to get out of the patient's face before she removed herself from patient. Needless to say, she was fired on the spot. The patient was petrified, and I calmed him down by reassuring him that he won't have to worry about that problem anymore or any other problem at the facility. I also apologized to him for what he just had experienced, and he was okay with that and smiled at me. I will never forget his calm smile; it made me feel better. Like I said before, we will all be judged when our number is up, and we don't want God to turn a blind eye to us on Judgment Day. Here is another poem for you I wrote.

Your Actions

Be careful of your actions in life.
You may not care what you do at one time
But sooner or later, your actions can make you walk the line.

Be careful what you say in life.
You may not care what you say at one time.
But sooner or later, your words can make you blind.
Be careful whose shoes you step on.
You may not care whose shoes they are.
But they may be an army of shoes that refuses peace and makes war.

Be careful of the heart you may break.
You may look back one day
And you made a mistake.
But then your true love has gone astray.
Be careful what you do and be careful what you say
'Cause you just may need that same person one day.

Let's move on to LTC number 3. Hurricane Katrina had hit fast and furious in New Orleans. I quickly signed up with two well-known volunteer organizations to help ASAP. Whoever picked me up first would have me as a volunteer nurse or any duties needed. One organization picked me up the first day I signed up, and the other picked me up right after that. So I was extremely busy, plus I had to work for a living to support my livelihood. We quickly started services the displaced New Orleans when they reached St. Louis, Missouri. I was told so many horror stories by the people we served.

I saw a lady sitting in the lobby, and I was compelled to go to her for some reason. After talking to her, she told me that with her in the lobby were three generations, and they were in the flooded water for three to four days. I saw worry and pain in her eyes, and my heart felt for her and her family. I got down on one knee and was drawn to kiss her hand. I told her that I was sorry but all the agencies are in this building to make her life better, and I will always remember her and pray for her and her family. There were so many stories that were horrific, but I maintained my professional composure and did what I had to do to help all the people as all of the volunteers did. At this volunteer building, I was the only black nurse there, and a Caucasian nurse was extremely prejudiced and displayed her dislike to me and our supervisor. The nurse quit 'cause she couldn't stand the idea of me being there. So you see, my friends, that some people volunteer from their heart and some volunteer for show. I wasn't going to quit 'cause I felt committed to the people in need.

At LTC number 3, my coworkers were livid (some of my coworkers) that I was working for free. They immediately took a hatred toward me, saying things like, "That bitch must think she's white. Only white people do what she is doing as a volunteer," "How could she work part-time and work full-time as a volunteer and afford to live?" Well, Jesus made sure I did not suffer at home and did not suffer as a volunteer. I was single and was doing fine with my lifestyle. I had a roof over my head, food in the kitchen, a car to drive, etc.

One day, when I clocked in at work, the air in the facility was thick with unsettled evil 'cause I could feel it. Later that night, a maintenance worker got on the house intercom system and yelled, "ALL THE LADIES IN THE HOUSE, SAY HEEEY, HOOOOOM HEEEEY, HOOOOO." I immediately counseled him, and he told me that I was just the supervisor over nursing, not maintenance. I told him, "My friend, when we're the only ones in the house and management is gone for the day, I'm over everything to see that this facility is run smoothly and professionally." He went over to tell his buddy (another nurse) what I said, and word spread like wildfire that President Bush (that was one of the many nicknames I was given by staff members) reprimanded him. So he and a group of nursing staff members decided to sit in the patients' dining room and use a rash of profanity, talking loud and acting like a group of hoodlums. All seven of them were fired the same night, including the maintenance worker.

As days passed, some of the staff members were angry 'cause their friends were fired. They didn't see the reason. They just wanted to add more hate in their hearts because I was doing the right thing. One of the nurses was on her way over from one side of the facility toward me I could feel she was getting ready to start chaos. This is what I had to deal with on a regular basis. I felt alone 'cause no one in my shift had the backbone to stand up to the staff members about their unprofessionalism. One stated that if she writes someone up, then they may do something to her car or treat them like I was treated. I was taken aback by their reasoning. But the nurse who was heading over to start chaos with me slipped and fell. Her legs went up in the air, and she landed on her buttocks and back rolled toward the wall, and her butt rolled her back into the middle of the floor. She was in a lot of pain. Her imitation fingernails broke off, and some of her fingers were bleeding badly. She got up and asked me if I saw her fall. As if she was angry at me 'cause she fell on her way to start problems with me. It was as if the Lord picked her up and slammed her on the floor and rolled her 'cause her feet was in a hurry to start evil. This is what happens when God is by your side 'cause He will protect you. One nurse told me that if I learned to turn my head as the others did that my trouble would stop. I responded in an unbelievable tone, "I'm not going to turn my head to let patients suffer when I have to face God on Judgment Day, and I don't want Him to turn His head away from me!" That conversation never transpired again. Please read Proverbs 15:32.

Moving on to LTC number 4. I worked at numerous LTCs because I chose to do so for my own personal reasons. The good thing about that was I took my own personal vacations at least four to five times a year, and those vacations were well needed and deserved. At least at 80 percent of the facilities I worked for I made sure that the staff had home-cooked meals from me, whether they appreciated it or not. But my containers were always empty when I got off duty, so

I'm sure it was excellent meals. Every holiday, I would cook holiday meals for my staff to show them I appreciated their work and to show them I cared. We all have to be held accountable for our sins on earth and heaven. So I didn't let a lot of things hold me back from continuously trying to do the right thing at work and at home. My home was kept peaceful 'cause I made it that way. Sometimes, after work, I would cook myself a steak on the grill. After working the second shift, I was usually home around 11:30 p.m. I got lonely sometimes, but I had to wait for the right man to come into my life. After two divorces, I wasn't in a hurry. I just took one day at a time.

One day, at work, a young lady who worked in dietary department came and sat next to me while I was outside having a cigarette break. She had softness in her demeanor and voice. She said that when the staff members see her talking to me, they're not going to like her anymore. But she doesn't care that she wished more nurses were like me. This made me feel better. I felt like an angel had touched her to come to me with kind words. So we sat and smoked cigarette together for the remaining five minutes of my break. She said, "You are a real good nurse that cares about people. If they all did this, it would be a better place to work." All I could tell her is that I'm working on their attitudes and hate and half doing their jobs and tasks.

LTC number 5. This particularly DON (director of nursing) wasn't mean or rude. Thank God for that. She told me that I intrigued her, so she went and talked to a psychic about me. I was appalled at this and tuned in to what she had to say. She said the psychic told her that I cannot change the world, and I told her that I'm not Jesus; only He can save the world, not I. I said, "Look, I volunteer 'cause it is a passion of mine that I share with others who need help. Even if I just helped one person, that's better than none." It says in the Bible that people should not go to fortune-tellers and psychics. It's against what God wants us to do. But I wasn't going to preach to her because her mind was made up. It was too eerie, so I quit that job the next day.

The truth is that I worked at so many LTCs that the numbers are beyond what I care to remember about. Neglect, abuse in all forms, unbecoming conduct, and staff infections happen in LTCs and in hospitals as well. Most of staff members in health care do not like washing their hands. I've even personally experienced this for my own health care. One day, in the emergency room, I asked a nurse if could she please wash her hands before giving me the pills that she was about to give to me. The nurse looked down at my feet and slowly looked up to my face and said that we don't have to wash our hands here, that we can use hand sanitizer, and she already did that before entering my treatment room. Then she got on the computer (computers hold a copious amount of germs) and, not washing her hands, handed the pills over to me and dropped them in my hand. I reported her to the hospital DON in person, and to this day, I have not received any feedback on that matter. Universal precautions are not being used by every individual health care worker.

Moving on to LTC number 6, this was not all, but it was the last of the LTC that I worked at. I was standing in the hallway, conferring with another nurse about a patient. The nurse I was talking to looked behind me, and without warning, another staff member ran into my hip with a stainless steel hospital food cart that made my body twist and bow forward. Its impact was so hard I was dizzy and almost passed out. When I regained my composure, I asked her why she hit me with the cart. Her response was, "I didn't even see you there" (her eyes were glazed). I took the proper steps in reporting this and making an incident report. Before this incident, I had a recent surgery on my knee, and this incident had reinjured my post-surgical knee, lower back, and hip. I was already seeing an attorney about this thrown-away incident and pain. My knee had swollen largely after this, and I could hardly walk, and the lower back pain was just as bad. My PCP (primary care physician) would not allow me back to work, and I had to apply for disability. Now I needed a total knee replacement.

That surgery went horribly wrong. When I woke up from the surgery, I noticed that my knee looked deformed with the way it was wrapped. I asked the surgeon what was wrong with my knee. He said, "Oh, nothing. It was just the swelling from the surgery." I didn't believe him and drifted off to sleep. After I was discharged for home, I couldn't walk. My knee had detached from the bones of my legs, and I was confined to a wheelchair.

Prior to the surgery, I had met a man who was also a nurse, and we had moved in together. I expressed genuine concern. But that's when he started plotting unbeknownst to me. I will call him Roger. Roger appeared to be a nice, caring, and loving person. Little did I know it was for his own personal gain. He was telling people that he couldn't work 'cause I was in a wheelchair. I told him that he has to work to pay the bills 'cause I couldn't work anymore. When Roger discovered that I was going to be awarded a compensation for the knee injury, he found every excuse not to work. He just wanted to lie around and be on the computer all day. There was no reason for him not to work for eight hours, five days a week. I was under so much stress. I finally stopped stressing myself out and told him one last time to get a job and stop making up excuses not to work.

He finally got a nursing job and called me at home one day from work, asking me when I would get awarded and if he could quit his job; and I told him no, that he had to work to keep the money flowing for the bills. All he could think about was my money that I would eventually receive. I didn't realize it at the time that money, being lazy, and drugs were what he really wanted to do.

My prosthetic knee had separated from my leg bones. I called my attorney and told him that my entire lower leg had twisted to the right instead of being in the front. I went and saw another doctor at another hospital to see if he could help me walk again. He examined me and scheduled me an appointment in the near future. The doctor had to scrape cement out of my leg and implant titanium rods in my upper and lower leg and a new prosthetic knee. I was able to walk the very next day after the surgery. Still insisting that Roger get a job 'cause I was permanently handicapped. He told me that it was hard for him to get a job 'cause he was caught stealing narcotics from a pharmacy, and he had a record. So I used my business contacts to land him a job. Roger called me from work and asked me if he could quit his job after I receive my award, and I told him no. He just hated to work. A lot of stuff I know now about him I didn't know then 'cause I was battling pain and trying to recover from the surgeries. We were together two years. Then I had to have back surgery to repair the ruptured discs in my back. He was collecting unemployment benefits, which helped financially. After the back surgery, I was in so much pain, but I diligently managed to do my activities of daily living. I refused to give up and fought any obstacles that came my way.

As months passed, Roger wanted to get married, but I didn't right away. Months later, I asked my PCP for a CT scan of my brain 'cause I felt there was an aneurysm in my brain, and the doctor refused two times to do so. On Thanksgiving Day in 2007, I looked in the mirror and discovered that one pupil was smaller than the other, and I knew I had a stroke. So I finished curling my hair and told Roger that I was going to the emergency room to get a CT scan of my brain without calling my doctor. He asked me why was I going to ER, and I told him I believe I had a stroke. He said, "How do you know?" I told him, "'Cause I was good in my field, and I do know how to assess." I worked alongside doctors for years and learned a lot from them. I also told him I believe I have an aneurysm. So Roger took me to the ER, and it was confirmed that I had an 8-mm aneurysm on the left side of my brain.

The next month, Roger and I were married, and I told him that with this huge aneurysm, we didn't have to get married 'cause I didn't know how long I had to live. That size aneurysm people normally don't or they would have a massive stroke among other things, and it would not be a good thing. But he wanted to marry anyway (because of the money I would receive). So we got married on December 7 (the day of infamy). That should have been a warning to me, but it didn't. I was too focused on a doctor (a well-seasoned doctor) that knew how to do brain surgery. My award finally came two weeks after I got married. I shopped for doctors, and I didn't see confidence in their eyes till I ran across one doctor that possessed confidence. I asked him how long I had to live (this was in January 2009). He told me two months. Wow, I said to myself. So I had to have brain surgery (craniotomy) in March.

I spent the next two months planning and trying to get things in order. Then the day came, March 18, 2009. The day of the brain surgery. I was admitted into the hospital that day. During the craniotomy while I was under anesthesia during the operation, my eyes opened, and I thought they couldn't see my eyes open. I thought it was one of the rare occasions I learned in nursing school—a patient wakes up and feels the surgical procedure. There was a loud sawing noise and a clinking noise. Actually, what happened was, I did not wake up. It was my spirit that separated from my body, and I could see every doctor and everything being done to my skull and brain. I thought to myself, *How could this be? How could I see all this and be alive?* In reality, I wasn't alive. The separation of my spirit from body had transpired. Then I realized I was no longer in my body and became afraid. I didn't know if I was going to heaven or hell 'cause it was a dark atmosphere as I was levitating above my body. When I became afraid, that's when I started levitating faster upward and landed in the Lord's arm. He cradled me like a baby. I felt joy, peace, love, and it felt like every molecule in my body was highlighted with the Holy Spirit. I stopped looking down at my body and told God that I wanted to stay with Him. I lay my head on His shoulder and went to sleep 'cause I was happy and was in peace. I was told after a week that I was in a coma, and when I woke up, I couldn't talk, but I remember my experience with God. That He let me remember. I didn't know my name, didn't know I was married, and I didn't know a lot of things in my past or present. My memory was a blank, but I still remember being in God's arm. He did not want me to forget that—that He is.

When the doctor asked me my name, I could not remember it. When they asked me what my husband's name was, I didn't even remember being married. It was a whirlwind of neverland for me to remember my life on earth. There was a speech therapist that was assigned to me in the hospital, and she was relentless in teaching me how to talk again. Half my head (the crown) was shaved bald. I had staples on my head from one ear all across the top of my head to the other ear. I had to start at preschool work in order for me to learn the small things in life like how to recognize things and how to read again. That preschool work was extremely hard to learn. I was like a child with the things of the world, trying to remember my life and all the things I knew before brain surgery.

Roger was a Caucasian male, so we were a mixed couple. Eventually, I remembered being married. He came every day, except for one day that he didn't visit me in the hospital. Later, I found out he was at home getting drugged out that day. He was an opportunist. A lot of things I didn't find out till after we were married. He hid his true self for two years till we were married. After marriage, the real him came out. He was planning on putting me in a home because of my brain surgery so he could spend my money on drugs and take control of my bank account. But little did he know they released me home after one week of brain surgery 'cause I had met the goals to go home. After going home, he showed me around the house to familiarize myself from what I used to know. I was scared because the atmosphere did not feel right to me. Little did I know it was him that wasn't right at that time. One time, I caught him in my panties and clothes, and I screamed. He ran off like a wolf in the woods. We had a creek wrapped around our house, and we lived on five to six acres of land.

He started planning on how to get rid of me. I couldn't do all the things I did before, so I didn't know how to add or subtract, balance a checkbook, or do anything I used to do. It took me almost two weeks to learn how to make coffee again. He wouldn't help me with it. I simply could not remember how to make coffee. After a few weeks at home, he would not pick up my prescriptions from the pharmacy. All he wanted to do was get high and sleep off with my money. He became violent afterward.

He would not sleep in the house; he would sleep out in the woods and creek and walk in the next morning muddy and wet. All this was scaring me, so I spent the night in a hotel the next day. When I returned home the next day, he was sitting at the dining room table. Roger had brown eyes, but that day, they were black with a deep shadow over them. He was looking crazy, and I was scared. He told me he was the devil, and I have no idea what was in his mind while staring at me. I thought to myself, *My god, I'm sitting across from the devil.* I made up an excuse to leave the house. I walked backward to the door. I remembered how to drive and I drove till I saw a police car and waved the policewoman down and told her what was happening in my house and that I found child pornography on his computer. She called for backup, and two male police officers came back to the house with me 'cause I was afraid he was going to shoot me with his shotgun. They arrested him and told me that there was a naked boy on his computer. The police took his computer with them along with discs and the desktop hard drive. I never wanted to involve my children to get hurt, but I had to tell them to help me move out of that house, and one of my children found a stack of pictures while moving me. The pictures consisted of children in porn acts. I was so hurt to see these children being exploited like that after the pictures were shown to me. It sickened me and made me angry. I found a little duplex house about thirty miles away and struggled to care for myself. Even though my children helped me, I was all alone with the horrific memories from the past with Roger.

Marriage and Trust

Marriage is a cherished partnership.
Trust is what adheres a marriage together.
You must trust each other,
Not just sometimes but forever.
If trust is ever broken
Between a woman and a man,
It shatters a relationship
That will no longer stand.
You cannot have harmony without trust.
Distrust leads to chaos in the home
Until, eventually, one day,
You're all alone.
Think about the consequences
That may occur before you commit a distrustful act,
Or you may ruin your relationship,
And that's a fact.
If your mind tells you it's wrong
And your heart steers you astray,
Put your mind and heart together.
This will lead you the right way.

All poems in this book are written by me to help teach, encourage, and inspire people about life. But all credit goes to God, who gave me the tools I needed to write this book.

After I moved away from Roger, he found out where I lived. He was always on the computer trying to ruin people whom he felt wronged him in the past and the future. He started stalking me through the mail. He was even telling people that he wrote my poetry books. I wrote those books years before I even met him with a copyright filed with the Library of Congress in Washington. Not only was he a liar, he was also very manipulative. The county where I turned all the evidence of his child porn over let the charges go, and he was free to harass and torment me. The county where I moved to was on his side and did not charge him with harassing or stalking me at my new residence in which I lived alone. If the law wouldn't do anything, who was I to turn to for help? He did things like write letters and made calls to agencies and even called the highway patrol to my residence based on lies to prohibit me from driving. He made it so that I had to take the driving test all over again. Nothing was done to stop this man from leaving me alone. He had stolen my money. I was only living off disability benefits. I was almost homeless, and I was hungry a lot 'cause his lies terminated all the benefits I was getting. He was a very convincing liar, and to think, he took an oath at nursing graduation, and he broke all the rules and falsely took an oath that he had no intentions to abide by. I was getting ready to get evicted from my home 'cause I had no money. After months of the police, social services, and other agencies not helping me, I had no choice but to move back to him 'cause I didn't want to be homeless. I could not live with my children because of the various reasons they had. I was still learning, and my brain never got a chance to heal as it should have because from the day I came home after the brain surgery, it was all pure havoc and hell. My brain could not handle all this, but I knew I had to survive.

As my memory started to increase, I remembered attorney secretary and my attorney. Between these two people, they were a solid rock in my life by listening and helping me when I needed someone to talk to. We had known one another for years due to my work-related injury that my attorney diligently worked on without flaw to make sure I got the help I needed. I remembered, when I was working as a nurse, that some of my patients were unable to speak and I had to be their voice. When I was in the hospital, I was force-fed a banana, and I am allergic to fresh fruit. But I could not speak and say, "Please don't feed me that 'cause it will cause me to have a copious amount of emesis." If my chart had been read, then the staff would have known this. After I was force-fed, the emesis started to build up in my stomach, and my head was so swollen I had to actually use my head to guide my body to roll over so I wouldn't get emesis in my lungs. I rolled over on my side eventually, and a vast amount of emesis began to gush out of my mouth. If I did not do this, it would build up in my lungs and I would have died. For some reason, I remembered a lot during my recovery period but could not speak for almost a week, I was told. I happy that I cared for my patients because I believe that Jesus saw my actions, and He cared for me. Here is another poem that I wrote after being a nurse for years and before all my surgeries came about.

Hidden Voice

My life is in your hands.
I'm fragile at my age.
I feel like a bird
Locked inside a cage.
I spread my wings to fly,
But there is nowhere to go.
Therefore, you are my sole caregiver.
Your wings carry me a flow.
You are my voice
Because I am unable to speak.
I depend on you every day,
Sometimes week to week.
You are my legs
When you transfer me

From wheelchair to bed.
You are the roots, and I am the tree.
You are my hands
When it is time to eat.
Look at my eyes.
I'm longing for that piece of meat.
You are my strength.
I depend on you for all my needs.
Examine my body language.
Please dress me up in those pretty beads.
You are the caregivers
Who help me when I'm ill.
You nourish me back to health
And get me over the hill.
I am the raft in the sea,
And you are the oar
That glide me to shore
And protect me from the tides that roar.
I am the voice that you do not hear.
I speak with my eyes
And, sometimes, through my tears.

As my brain was slowly healing, I was trying to think how I could get away from Roger and get a divorce. I was afraid because the police departments had failed me and let him walk away. I had no protection, so I had to protect myself. When he hit me, I fought back as hard as I could. He thought he had me where he wanted me because he knew that I had another award coming to me. We just didn't know when. He started using drugs again, and it was the same old thing. When the drugs started to wear off him, he always became violent and crazy. He was an obsessive, manipulative, evil, conniving, and revengeful person. He would stalk his exes from the past by the computer. The computer was an obsession to him as well.

When I became financially able, I left his apartment and moved into a house in a different county. He broke his lease and followed me to the new house. He told me that if I did not let him move in that he would have me committed into an institution. He had already been telling friends and family, behind my back, that I was crazy and the reason he couldn't work 'cause he had to be with me to watch and take care at all times, which was a lie. He did nothing but sleep, stay on the computer, and do drugs. This was just an excuse so he didn't have to work, for he was lazy and crazed with drugs since he was twelve years old. I discovered a lot of things he did in the past before we were married. Roger told me that I know what he was capable of doing and he would do it again. I didn't know how to get rid of him. It was like I was trapped in an unwanted marriage, and I wanted out of it. I went to the doctor one day, and when I returned, he had my clothes on and had white powder under his nose. I didn't care what he did to me, so I called the police.

Finally, I lived in the right county where the police did help me. He was arrested for slamming my hand in the door because he was high and he wanted to take over my possessions and the house. He broke the restraining order many times and was arrested each time. I was so happy that the police took me seriously. The police found his shotgun and an arsenal box of shotgun shells locked in his office. He was planning a murder suicide, and God stopped it. I immediately filed for divorce within a week, and we were divorced six months later. The police took his shotgun away with them. Roger was not supposed to have a gun 'cause of his past record. But some gun shop sold him one anyway. He was supposed to show up in court for the harassment and stalking charges, but he never showed up for his court date. The assistant district attorney told me the judge had put a bench warrant out on him, and he was facing some years for this no-show.

He continued to track me down via Internet and obtained my phone number. He even e-mailed me a nigga letter, which was turned over to the police, among other things as well. He was a habitual stalker and harasser. He used to brag about how he obtained and harassed people in the past. So I knew I was dealing with an unstable person. He kept driving by my house and circling my home, so I had to move out of my house for my own protection. He harassed me for almost two years till, eventually, one day, he stopped. I knew that it would not last for long. He stole my identity and opened an account in my name. When I found this out, I had the agency cancel it and explained that he knew all my personal information. He is not the kind of normal person to let go and move on. I didn't sleep with him for the past two years. I slept in the reclining chair. He was disgusting to me, and I didn't want him near me. I was so happy I was finally divorced and had gotten rid of him. I learned how to balance my checkbook, among other things, as my brain healed. My brain was never going to heal or feel at peace as long as he was in my life.

To this day, and to my knowledge, the police have not found him yet for the bench warrant. He is still somewhere out there, doing evil things to people. I had to cut some of my friends out of my life because they were listening to him tell lies about me behind my back. Therefore, I could not trust some of my old friends anymore 'cause it takes two to talk and to listen, and they never once told me what he was doing behind my back. A true friend would tell or warn me of his plans about what he was going to do to me, and I didn't know why they were taken in by him.

I have a new life now, and it is peaceful. I continue to be a volunteer nurse when I can, but I still have to look over my shoulder till he is put in jail. Roger told me once that if his shotgun wasn't taken away from him that he was going to use it on himself, then I knew him well. He was planning on taking me out with him with a shotgun blast. There is a thin line between love and hate, and he hated me for consistently asking him for a divorce. He has a psychotic mind, which is very dangerous. After we were divorced, it took many months for me to recover mentally for what I had been through with him. But my memory and healing power is so much better, and it feels good to feel free of his wrath. He even sent me an e-mail, saying he was going to boil me death. That e-mail was given to the best police department there is that helped protect me. He was unable to lie to and manipulate this particular police department.

He was calling everyone I knew after stealing my telephone numbers and storing them in his computer. The true friends ignored his calls, and the false friends accepted his call. He was afraid of men, but not afraid of women. He was a real coward in his life. He even told me about that he was planning on killing his father for his fortune but changed his mind. He talked about taking revenge and thought of killing his exes. Imagine living in a house with a psychotic, pathological, and manipulative evil person. I had to get away from him and had to divorce him, hoping that would stop the madness in his sick mind. But it didn't.

Even after our divorce he had the audacity to text me and ask me if we could be friends, which was another violation of the restraining order. I turned that evidence over to the police. He called my best friend out of town and told her he was coming to her house. That friend was scared out of her wits. So I called the police and let them talk to her via telephone. The police officer was furious with Roger with all this habitual harassment on me and others. Another police complaint was filed against him, terrifying my friend out of town. He thought that this police department was going to go easy on him with his smooth lies as he was able to convince other departments not to prosecute him. Oh, he was real good at being a convincing smooth liar. A person doesn't get like this overnight, so he had to be like this all his life. He just hid it well, especially with the women. Plus his family had been telling me things about him after we were married.

When we were separated before our divorce, I learned later that he was so strung out on drugs that he was standing naked by the river and was arrested. Drugs is a big problem for some people, and it can drive them to hurt others or themselves. This is not the life I was going to live in. I struggled for years, trying to get back the memory and all the things I used to know. Now that he was out of my life, I could concentrate on straightening my life out, and even that was a struggle. Inside, I was afraid to be involved in another relationship, and I avoided it. It's been over two years after my divorce, and it was a rough two years trying to avoid my ex and get my life back on track. I lived for one and a half years with family or friends to avoid my ex tracking me. It wasn't easy, but I did what I had to do to protect myself. After that, I settled into a one-bedroom apartment. I discovered that my ex had stolen my identity and opened a credit report in my name so he could track what I was doing. As soon as I found out, I wrote to the company and sent them documents to prove who I am, and they discontinued the forged account immediately. Like I said, Roger has been doing this to people for decades, which was unbeknownst to me till I had to go through it. Every doctor I had since we were married, he always had to get the same doctor for himself in order to tell lies and discredit me. A friend told me that he was setting me up to be committed so he could take over everything I had and owned. He never had anything in life, so this was his way of getting what he never had. Even if it meant tormenting an innocent victim of his craziness.

Don't Give Up

Reach far, climb high, and soar above.
Never give up on your dreams.
Work at it diligently.
Things are not as hard as they seem.
Live your life to its fullest extent.
Continue to excel.
Don't give up.
Hold on, and life will treat you well.
No need for pondering on things that were meant to be.
Instead, concentrate on the next phase
And cling to your strategy.
Do not succumb to a haze.
Put one foot in front of the other.
Continue to walk without stumbling.
Good, strong, sturdy strides are of confidence,
And steadiness brings on wings.
Don't give up.
Think negative and that is where you will stay.
Think positive and it will take you a long way.
Fly like the eagle and soar with precision.
Strong, sturdy wings are very graceful.
Don't give up.
Being positive is very delightful.

No matter what your situation is, please don't give up. There is always hope, and when you have hope, there is a rainbow waiting ahead for you. Many times, I felt like giving up, but God pushed me and made sure that I sustained my faith, hope, love, and trust. All the things I've encountered in life. If I can make you, then you must have the courage, faith, and hope to continue as well. If you're caught up in a bad situation, just remember that the Lord is always there and His angels will protect you from harm.

Roger said that I would never divorce him, and if I tried, he would make my life miserable. He even harassed his own mother when he was angry with her. He sent agencies and the highway patrol to her house to have her committed, stating she is incapable of taking care of her herself and her house. I thought if he would stoop so low to do this to his own mother, then I knew what I had coming. This is why I had to proceed with my divorce as quickly as possible. He had family members tell me that he would cross-dress when he was high on drugs, and they saw him naked when the drugs kicked in.

Even though it took two years for us to get married, he hid his craziness well. Even I didn't see it till after we were married. This is what you call a wolf in a sheep's clothing, except he was worse than a mean wolf. He was an evil psychotic thing. That spent his life revenging people whom he became obsessive with when they threw him out of their lives. He only felt like a real man when he had a shotgun; otherwise, he wouldn't face a man, only women. This makes him a coward in my eyes. If you're ever in a relationship or married and it's havoc, get out while you can 'cause some men will kill you before they let you leave. One never know what goes in another person's mind, but use your instincts and get away. I met a man (a real man) about a year ago. At first I was skeptical, but he treats me like no other man has before—with love, respect, and an astronomical amount of wisdom planted within him. I will not mention his name. I wrote a poem for him and asked if it was okay to print it in this book, and he said yes. Because this is how I feel about him. Finally, a man who appreciates me for who I am and there is no ulterior motive involved.

The Man I Love

He's a man who can see
Right through me.
He knows my heart and ways.
When I hide my feelings, he can still see.
See me for who I am,
Love me for the person I am.
Makes me laugh at small things
As I spread his toast with jam.
I love to make him happy,
And I love to please him.
Even when he's ill, he's never crappy.
His heart is made of peace and love.
His knowledge is astronomical.
You would have to see what I see, which is a dove.
He has stolen my heart
And he has stolen my love.
He is the last man I will ever be with
'Cause there is no other dove.
This strong beautiful dove is mine.

So you see, there is life after everything and even life after death, for which I have experienced. Both of it is a blessing to live and write about it. I have known him for a few years as a friend. We were friends before, which made our relationship strong with an unbreakable bond. Some things I can write about, but my true love is private and that's the way I want to keep it.

I am putting myself back together—heart, mind, body, and soul. There's an old saying that the eyes are the window to the soul. I say, only God can see the soul and humans can't. But the eyes are the window to the heart. You can see a lot through a person's eyes with good eye contact and see their intentions from the heart of things. I don't confess to know everything 'cause I don't. I can only write and talk about my personal experiences in life and with intentions of helping others as well.

As a child, I could see things just like my mother could. One day, she asked me if I heard screaming in the basement where we lived. I told her yes, and my other siblings didn't hear it. My mom turned to me and said, "You believe me, don't you?" I answered yes, and there was no one in the basement. Only she and I could hear it. I guess I had the same instincts she had. We both could see things (people) that you could see right through them. I guess you could say spirits. It really petrified me 'cause I was only a young girl. I covered my face every time I see things. Sometimes, I would have dreams that would come true; this terrified me.

One day, a neighbor called me over to her, and she told me, "You can see and feel things, can't you?" I replied yes, and then she told me not to be afraid of it, that it was a gift. I said that I don't want that gift. The lady said that when she was young, she used to be afraid of the things she saw and heard but learned it was a gift, and eventually, she wasn't afraid anymore. She said that she saw this in me a long time ago, and she felt it was time she told me. Even though my mother had told me the same thing, I didn't feel any better about it. Sometimes, I would tell my best friend, Ellen, about my dreams, and she would witness it come true within the same week. She became frightened and told me never to dream about her and not to tell me anymore of my dreams. So I gave her that respect and never repeated my dreams to her anymore. She was a good friend, and I didn't want to frighten her any more than she was already was.

It wasn't easy being able to see things I didn't want to see in some people's eyes. But I must admit, it saved my life many times and others' as well. I'm not a psychic or anything like that, but I have strong intuitions most of the time. But one thing God never let me forget was being in His arms after brain surgery. For the rest of my life, I will remember the touch of the Holy Spirit. It felt like every molecule in my spirit was filled with happiness, joy, love, and peace 'cause peace is from God, and I was blessed to experience this closeness with Him. The Lord is what saved me from Roger's craziness and abuse. Abuse can come in all types such as: physical, mental, verbal, and much more, including emotional. Just think about it. A person comes home from not knowing her name to a world of hell with the person she was married to. I could feel the evil from him when I came home. One week after being discharged from the hospital, the house was in a disarray, and I had to figure out how to clean again when I should have been in bed resting and not being abused. This only slowed down my healing process. In the hospital, even though I was in a coma, I could hear even though I couldn't speak, and I could understand even though the staff and family thought I couldn't.

My friends, if you ever have a friend or a loved one in the hospital, keep talking to them because you can hear, and this helps the healing process. Then the doctors had to put a clip inside my brain to obliterate the aneurysm in order for me to live. The doctor was a brilliant brain surgeon in order to do this delicate life-threatening operation. I still have some problems with memories and such, but I came a long way. If you saw me, one would not think I have been through a series of surgeries, including brain surgery. This was a miracle 'cause God loves to create miracles so that others can see and believe in Him as well. Miracles happen every day; we just don't see them and some are seen by Him.

A pastor once called me a walking miracle 'cause most people don't survive or have other visible symptoms that can be seen. Just because some people call themselves pastors that doesn't mean that they are true pastors. Another pastor had spread rumors that the reason I was having so many surgeries is because God was punishing me. What a silly misinformed so-called Christian he was. He would have made himself look better if he had said, "Look, God blessed her to come through all these surgeries. What a miracle." Instead he was a judgmental and gossiping hypocrite. There are even people that attend church every Sunday, and they can be the biggest devil there is. As my mother used to say sometimes, the devil can be sitting right next to you in church.

After all some bad experiences I've had in various churches, I decided to let the Lord be my church every day of the week. With Him, you can't go wrong. I look back in my life, and I can remember some things that I don't want to remember. I had this step-uncle that had convinced my mother, when I was about seven years old, to let me come over to his house and spend some time with me. I was afraid of him. I don't really know why, but my spirit didn't feel right being alone with him for some reason. My mom told me to go spend some time with my step-uncle, and he tried to make me eat some stewed rabbit. I refused to eat it and started crying even though he kept trying to make me eat it. I was thinking to myself that I wanted to go home. So I stood up and looked him directly in the eyes and said, "Take me home!" He tried to console me from crying by hugging me, and he stuck his tongue inside my mouth. I spit his tongue out and screamed, and he said he would take me home and he did. After he left, I told my mother what he did, and she didn't believe me, and that broke my heart. But the only way I could get out from going over to his house and making my mother not let me go with him was to cry hard and scream no, no, no! That would get me out of that situation of having to go over his house again.

What he did to me was sickening, and I hated to see him come over our house, and he would look at me a lot. I didn't like that either 'cause I was thinking he was going to try and stick his tongue in my mouth again if we were ever left alone. So I always avoided that man. How can a seven-year-old kid make her own mother believe her that what he did was disgusting and it terrified her? I wonder, to this day, how many other kids he has done this to even though he is dead now. No child should experience any type of abuse 'cause it can be devastating in the long run of their life. I already had a sibling who tried something disgusting with me, and I was too little to find the right words. But I told my mother about it, and she didn't believe that either. I thought, *Who am I to go to if my own mother, who is supposed to be my protector, don't believe me?*

So when I became a teenager, I grew taller than everyone in the house, and there were a lot of fighting with siblings in the household. Usually end up with my winning 'cause I turned out to be more physically fit than they were. I couldn't be and wouldn't be pushed around or abused again 'cause I made it that way. Although they would lie and say I started the fight, which wasn't true, but my mother always believed them over me. I once told my mom that a sibling put a knife to my throat, and nothing was done about that either. Then another sibling threw a knife at me, and it stuck me in the temple and I fell out. I had to get stitches for that, and my mom told me to tell the doctor that I fell down the steps or she would put me in a home. When the doctor asked me away from my mother how I got the cut, I just started crying 'cause I was tired of the abuse. The doctor said, "You didn't get a deep cut by falling down the steps." He left the treatment room and yelled at my mother. I thought I was going to a home after that, but she didn't send me away as I thought she would. Nothing was done by my mom for the sibling that stabbed me. All I could think of, *When I get older, I'll stop all this myself.* Which I did as I became a teenager. The siblings no longer had the best of me. I got the best of them from years out as I grew. I didn't have a happy childhood, but I made the best of it for whatever it was worth.

Falling Down

I fell and scraped my knees.
Please help me back to my feet.
God is surely watching you
So please help me to my seat.
Help me brush off the dirt.
God will surely reward you.
My ankle is too weak to move.
One day you may need my help too.
Never think twice about helping someone.
Going once! Going twice!
Help is not an auction,
And it is not a game of dice.
Do goodwill for all,
And He will never let you fall.
Life is so great!
He blessed us with many gifts.
Grasp at it with all your heart.
Stand together and not apart.

Proverbs 24:16

"For a righteous man may fall seven times and rise
again, but the wicked shall fall by calamity."

Proverbs is one of my favorite books in the Bible 'cause it
teaches, guides, and promotes wisdom to everyone.

The Heart

The heart doesn't lie.
It holds the inner self of who you are.
You cannot be what you are.
You cannot be what you are not meant to be.
Either it's of peace
Or it's of war.
Especially if it shines like a golden fleece.
If your heart is of war,
You cannot find peace within yourself.
A chaotic heart leads to despair,
Collecting dust upon a shelf.
Peace is of God and from God.
He'll plant seeds in your heart
That will not only benefit you
But others as well, right from the start.
When the heart is free, it grows constantly.
Doors begin to open widely.
As you look through the doors with awe.
With contentment, you are where you were striving to be.

After all the trials and tribulations I had to go through in life,
self-discipline, will, determination, and dedication are what got
me through life and life's bumps along the way. When Roger and I
worked together, he wasn't much of a charge nurse or supervisor. He
was afraid to write staff up or to delegate staff to do their job. When

we were married, I discovered he wasn't much of a man or a husband. He hid his insanity till after we were married. He had no furniture, only personal belongings, which wasn't much. A week after we got married, he put his arms around me and said, "Now everything you got I've got." That's when I realized he married me for his own gain. I had to have brain surgery in a couple of months, and that was the only thing on my mind. So I so much as shrugged off his statement at that time. Little did I know it would get worse and worse. He hit me on the head one week after being discharged from the hospital where I had the aneurysm at. He was high on drugs, and I was afraid of his shotgun 'cause he wasn't in his right mind and he wasn't the man that I had married. I quickly came back with the police, and he was arrested. Because of the child porn that was found in his possessions. He harassed me and stalked me on a nonstop basis afterward. He would be out wet and muddy in the woods at night or on the computer all night and sleep all day like a house pet.

One night, I woke up in the middle of the night and saw him on the computer; he quickly turned it off. I asked what he was doing on the computer. He replied, "I was talking online with some kids, and they don't know anything about hell." Even though my brain was still healing, I knew this was weird, and I started watching him. One day, I was looking for my potato-peeling knife, and I couldn't find it. I found it a few days later under the bathroom rug accidently. I brought it to his attention. He said the handle was good for crushing up pills and sniffing them. I knew I had to get away from him. He took advantage of my surgery, trying to learn things all over again. He was cocky, mean, and angry. He thought he had it made for the rest of his life with me. Little did he know I would regain my memory and leave him permanently and file for a divorce. The excuse he used to tell people that I had brain surgery and I was crazy so he couldn't work in order to take care of me was a lie. He wouldn't even show me how to remember to make coffee, and he did not assist me with anything around the house. All he did was sleep off his drug habits. It was a long journey learning things I used to know, but I managed to get it back. I couldn't get my family involved because I was afraid they would get hurt or killed.

Roger talked about his shotgun every day and would keep it in wherever room he was in. He was insanely sewn to his shotgun. He felt powerful with it and powerless without it. He would walk around in his pajamas every day after he was approved for disability like he was Hugh Hefner. He thought he was a cocky big shot. All he did was eat, sleep, use the bathroom like a domestic animal. It made me angry and sick of looking at him, and I told him so. I didn't care if he didn't like it 'cause it was the truth. I was tired of arguing and fighting every day, so I asked him to move out. The last time I had him arrested, the police wouldn't help me. But this time, the right police did help me and arrested him. I tried to hurry up and get a divorce while he was locked up in jail. But my attorney misplaced some of my paperwork and it took me six months to get a divorce instead of three months.

Men and women, don't ever think that you are stuck in a marriage 'cause there is always a way out before things get very sour. Be diligent, firm, and consistent and you can get rid of your worst half. He was trying to mold himself into me, it seems. Whenever I wrote poetry, he tried to write poetry, when I volunteered, he wanted to volunteer, and when I bought a guitar, he wanted to learn to play a guitar. Everything I did he wanted to do. It's as if he had no goals, dreams, or hopes in life. I told Roger to stop copying off me and figure out what he wanted to do in life for himself. I was tired of him tagging around me, listening, and watching everything I did. I told him I'm a woman and you're a man, go and do some man things and stop trying to copy me. It was irritating. Of course, he got angry, but I didn't care anymore about it or him. I just wanted out of the marriage and to get rid of him once and for all. I never wanted to see him again as long as I lived, I told him this. I never talked behind his back. I would tell him to his face. He talked about me with lies behind my back to friends, family, and anyone who would listen. He had no backbone, but he only had a backbone when he used to own a shotgun. He thought he was tough with it. He was obsessed with guns and with me.

Well, even after the divorce, he harassed me and stalked me. He even sent e-mails with *nigga* in it. Why would a white man marry a black woman then call her the N-word? I guess he was insane, jealous, and divorced. He said he would never let me get a divorce. Well, I did, and that was one thing he couldn't stop no matter what he did to me. I was adamant on divorcing him, and I did. The harassment went on for about two years of my life after the divorce. He didn't care about breaking the restraining order, and he didn't care about going to jail because of it. I was no longer afraid and called the police every time he sent me an e-mail or called me. I got tired of changing my telephone number, so I just let it be 'cause, somehow, he would always get the number. I also shut down my e-mail account so he would leave me alone. After all, anyone who plans to kill his own father and harass his mother and family didn't care whom he hurts. He told me once that he had planned to kill his ex-wife. I was taking all this in 'cause I knew what would be in store for me. He knew I couldn't swim, so he tried many times into taking me to the beach. I knew he would try and drown me, so I always refused to go.

When he saw everything was hopeless in trying to keep me married, I believe he planned a murder suicide for me. He even told me once that he would blow his head off if he ever had to go to jail, and I knew he was going to try and take me with him and whoever else was around. When the police saw an arsenal of shotgun shells right before I had him arrested, the officer took his shotgun away. Whoever sold him that shotgun was not supposed to 'cause I discovered he had a felony before we were married. He had stolen some narcotics from the pharmacy, and he was caught and sent to trial. He would only do probation for that. Sometimes, I thought he got away with a lot of dirt 'cause he was white and I was black. I lived it so I can say that. The first and the second police municipality did nothing to him, but the third municipality did do something about it. I thank God for those police officers at the third municipality for that. They really went out of their way to protect me, and I will always be grateful for that. It's been months now, and I haven't heard from that maniac, and I am happy about that. He made my life a living hell on earth. The things I had to go through, no one deserves that. I would have been set for life throughout my retirement, but he spent my money like it was his 'cause I couldn't count when I was released home from the hospital. It brings me much anxiety when I think about him or talk about him 'cause he was a devious devil. Sometimes, I know he drugged me 'cause of the way I would feel. So I stopped eating or drinking the things that he would rarely bring me. I have flashbacks of some of the things, but they are blurry to me.

Attorney secretary was someone I could talk to when I had problems; she was always nice and attentive when I would call, and my attorney figured out that the abuse happened after my brain surgery. He is a very smart man, and one of the best attorneys in the country in my opinion. He was always there to lend an ear as well, which kept me strong and kept me pushing on in life. I later discovered that Roger tried to turn me and my attorney against each other behind our backs. He was good at trying to turn people against each other. But it didn't work with my attorney and I and a few other people. Roger told me that an old girlfriend of his over a decade ago that he still held a grudge against her 'cause she didn't want him anymore. He talked about how he used to harass her and things he wanted to do to her. I think he was telling me all these things to put fear into me if I ever left him. Well, not only did I leave him, I also divorced him, and I can smile at that because I am free.

I remember having a dream about my mother; she was in a coffin. I had this dream one or two weeks before she died. I shrugged the dream off and knew it wouldn't come true, but it still bothered me. I asked my sister what it means when you dream of someone close to you die in your dream. I was hoping she would say, "Oh, nothing. It's just a dream." But in a week or two, my mom did die. It petrified me because the clothing she had on at the funeral home was the same clothes in my dream. As I stared at her in the funeral home wake, it was so hard to believe she died and left me. She died of aneurysm without insurance money to bury her with. But Jesus made it possible for the siblings and through donations to come up with the money to bury her with. I do miss her, and I'm happy we became best friends at the last year of her life. I have that to hang on to and remember. Statistics show that one out of fifteen people have aneurysm, and don't know it. I didn't find this out till years later. After my mother's death, that was one of the reasons I became a nurse. So no one I loved would die if there was help for them and to take care of others as well. I did the best I could do and followed the rules in nursing to provide excellent nursing care to all my patients. While in the limousine, my sister asked me about the dream I told her about a couple of weeks ago. She asked, "The dream you were telling me about, was it about Mama?" I answered yes in a grieving tone. She said, "You should have told us so we could have been looking out for her!" I didn't even answer her. I just looked at her, and then I think she knew how stupid it sounded. I'm not God and I'm not a psychic, so the heck with all this nonsense. Here's a poem I wrote after my mom expired.

An Awakening Dream

Once I had a dream,
A dream that felt like it was real.
And when I had awakened,
My world stood still.
I dreamed of my mother
Wearing a black dress with long sleeves,
With one bold white stripe.
I heard the rustling of the leaves.
My mother was lying down
As tears filled my eyes.
Then I realized that she had passed.
I looked up in the heavenly skies.
Asking God why.
My heart was very saddened.
I never said goodbye.
The dream had disturbed me.
Dreams come and dreams go.
The dream eventually left my thoughts
My spirits were no longer low.
As weeks went on, my mom did pass away.
Suddenly, the dream had returned to me.

I knew then, God was preparing me,
Preparing me for what was going to be.
My siblings and I miss Mom dearly.
We found peace among one another.
God had brought our family together,
With all sisters and brothers.
How strange it is for sisters and brothers
To live in the same town
And yet not really visit one another
Until something sits them down.
Love one another and never take life in haste
Because you may look back one day
And think what a waste.

I wrote this poem when I was interviewed on radio station. It was about my mother.

Mom

My mother was a strong woman,
A woman who has seen a lot.
She was also an excellent mom.
There was always food in the pot.
Sometimes it's hard to write about Mom.
I guess because I miss her so much.
My mom passed away years ago.
I do miss her motherly touch.
We shared tears and laughs.
We shared good and bad times.
We had good times on the front porch
Listening to the wind chimes.
When I feel low in spirits,
I remember the wise conversations we shared.
My heart cries out
When I think of how much she cared.

Dear Mom, I love you dearly.
I love you with all my heart.
Continue to pray for me, Mom
You've been my rock from the start.
You wiped my tears away
Whenever I cried.
You always knew when I was truthful,
And you knew when I lied.
You chased away bullies
When I was in grammar school.
You were always there.
You taught me the golden rule.
You were present to guide me
Through my teenage years.
When I was scared,
You chased away my fears.
How can I thank you
For giving me the breath of life?
But most importantly, I thank you
For teaching me to deal with life's strifes.

Even when Mom and I didn't get along for many years growing up, I always tried to respect her because she was my mother.
God said, "Honor your mother and father." This is one of the
Ten Commandments. Being raised in Catholic schools, the
Commandments were drilled to us in school. We even had a religion
class in school, which we were graded on as well. We went to church
each school day before lunch five days a week and on Sundays five—
you may as well say six—days a week. When I grew older as a young
adult, I chose my own Christian faith that I was comfortable with. As
I grew older, I became more involved in the Bible. I had Bible study
with my children and grandchildren. I taught them about God,
Jesus, and the Holy Spirit. Eventually, as they became young adults, I
started to read the Bible on my own to understand more what I read.
I asked Jesus to give me the understanding and knowledge on what I

read, and He did. We've all made mistakes in life and did things that were wrong, but He forgives us as we are supposed to forgive others.

Mistakes

Mistakes can happen to anyone.
You can learn from mistakes you make
By not doing them twice.
This is good advice to take.
Mistakes are not meant to torment you.
They are meant to teach you,
Or they can make you a better person.
They can bring you from old to new.
You can teach others from your mistakes,
Or you can even build from them.
Pondering on mistakes
May plunge your wits.
Stay sharp and focused, teach others what you've learned.
This may prevent others from taking the wrong turn.

I often think of our men and women in the military. They hold a special place in my heart and thoughts. I was planning a fund-raiser for the USO. That fell through because I was married at the time and was going through a tremendous amount of stress in every form, and I couldn't concentrate on what needed to be done while I had that man living under the same roof. But I do volunteer for various organizations as often as I can. This gives me a sense of fulfillment to my heart, mind, and soul. The military and veterans have seen things our eyes have not seen, and they have courage straight to the heart. I can't say enough good things about our men and women, active and nonactive, 'cause they all deserve the utmost respect and help that we can give them. Every war that has been fought abroad. Our brave men and women go without hesitation to protect us and protect others. When we see our brave men and women in uniform, always thank them for their services that they so selfishly give to us all.

I'm not sure where my driving inner self came from. I can only think of God Himself because I really fought mentally to come back (after God sent me back) after brain surgery. I was so frustrated when I had lost my voice during that time. When I did begin to speak again, most of the time I would say no when I wanted to say yes, and sometimes when I would say yes, I wanted to say no. It's amazing how the human brain is made. I only wished I had continued my education in medicine. But I couldn't afford to do so thus far in my life. Sometimes, I wish I should have worked harder to pursue further education in medicine as an MD. But everything happens for a reason in life, and I guess this was the path that was chosen for me. So always try and make the best of yourself and teach family, friends, and others what you've learned. So they too can meet their full potentials in life itself and pass along the torch to others in our lives.

Since I've been retired, I now spend my life volunteering, helping with fund-raisers, writing, and doing art paintings. I still love to cook as always, but I don't cook as much as I used to unless I have company or visitors over. Sometimes, I'll cook and share with neighbors, and the neighbors always commended me on the taste of my cooking, which made me feel good 'cause I made someone happy on those occasions. Many people contacted me and told me that my writing helped them in some of their decisions in life from my past poetry books, and my acrylic paintings always brought joy to others and helped raise money for people in need. This is basically what I'm really made of—helping and serving people, plus tidbits of teaching to some.

I honestly do miss having the bimonthly services I used to teach when I was working. Even if the in services only touched a few, it was better than none at all. I always tried to teach through my heart, mind, and soul, so it would stick with those who were willing to learn and listen. Several years ago, there was a vast electrical outage, and since I had already signed up with a variety of organizations, I showed up at a cooling shelter to offer my assistance. There were so many people to serve that it made me reach out to nurses and doctors that I knew on a personal level to come and help 'cause it was hard to do this all alone. No one returned my calls to help at the cooling shelter. So I went on and serviced the people and did the best I could. With my detailed nursing assessments, I had to send some people to the emergency room from the shelter. Illnesses consisted of high blood pressure, heat exhaustion, and everything in between illnesses you could think of. I didn't feel like I was too good to help people to bathroom, set up cots, or whatever I needed to do to get the job done and the people taken care of. I also had to hold a meeting for everyone in the shelter. The captain of the shelter looked at me and said, "What's wrong?" I told her I needed to hold a meeting about universal precautions because what I was seeing were germs that were going to spread and make others sick. I held the meeting with everyone via microphone. I heard some giggling in the crowd, and I addressed that right away, letting them know that this was a serious situation and to not take it lightly. In fact, listening can prevent illness or worse. The giggling stopped right after I announced that.

We Will Never Forget

(A Breakfast Prayer for 9/11)

There is nothing more important than family and friends
Sharing time together and eating together,
To have time for one another
No matter the season or the weather.
We thank you, dear Lord Jesus Christ,
For giving us this day
To spend together
And hear us as we pray.
We ask you, dear Lord,
To continue to bless our friends and family every day.
We ask for strength and guidance
And to mold us Your way.
We pray for the victims of the terrorist attacks,

Their families, and the rescue workers too.
We pray for our president and his officials
For their decisions that affect the old and new.
We pray for our parents and loved ones
Who have joined you in the past.
We thank you for opening doors,
For you are the first and the last.
You are the Alpha and the Omega
Who loves us no matter what our flaws may be.
You are the roots of our tree.
Keep us with you, dear Lord,
And never let us go.
Without your light,
There will never be a glow.
The light of life,
You've blessed us with indeed.
Keep our families under your dome,
For today we have planted a seed.
A seed that will sprout and grow
To a beautiful flower
In which we had to sow.

My warmest thanks to my attorney for his excellence in law as he worked for years to make sure I was compensated for my injury at work. After years of being in touch, he and his secretary were always available when I needed a friend to talk to. They were there in every storm I experienced throughout the years. My love and deepest thanks for that special anonymous man in my life who helped me and loves me for who I am for over the past few years. That part of my life about my new love remains private. Thank you for reading and purchasing this book, *The Silent Patient: A True Story*.

Closing

I worked till my left knee swelled so bad and hurt in excruciating pain that I could not walk anymore, with all of my weight bared down on my right leg. The doctor would not release me to go back to work due to my left knee and my lower back. I could not walk on both legs without falling sometimes. Being in constant pain for four long agonizing years, people could not tell that I was in pain at all times. I made it that way. It's surprising what you can do with the human mind and the spiritual guidance that God so freely gives to us all.

I found an orthopedic surgeon to do a much-needed total left knee replacement in 2007. This doctor had been a surgeon for almost all his adult life and was very experienced in knee replacement. People that I had spoken to had boasted on how excellent a surgeon this doctor was. So I felt pretty confident that the surgery would turn out well and that it would be a success. I will call him Dr. Martin. My first visit to Dr. Martin went well, and everything was explained to me. Little did I know that this would be the first of many journeys that I would have to endure—some for the good and some for the bad. But when it is one's time to walk any particular line, it is up to that individual. It is entirely up to them whether they walk it or crawl it or lie down on it and stop there on a dime. My husband and I both agreed, in the presence of Dr. Martin, that we would allow him to do the left knee replacement.

Surgery was done that following week, and when I woke up from the anesthesia, Dr. Martin was standing over my bed and asked me how I felt. I immediately looked down at my left knee all bandaged up from the surgery, and it did not look right to me. It looked abnormal. The swelling on the front of my left knee and the side of that knee was off. I asked Dr. Martin what was wrong with my leg, and he said, "It's just the swelling. It will go down." Then he sat on the side of my bed and said, "Most knee replacements only last about five years, but I did extra reinforcement on your replacement and gave reinforcement that you will not need one till another ten years." I said, "Thank you, Dr. Martin."

The doctor placed his hand on my right leg and smiled and said, "You're very welcome, Darlene, and you are my kind of woman." I thought to myself, *What the heck does he mean?* I quickly threw it away from my mind and went to sleep. It was hard to go to sleep 'cause the pain in my surgical knee was overwhelming. But eventually, I did drift off to sleep as a result of my post-op.

Was a successful and experienced nurse in gerontology. She worked as a charge nurse, supervisor, case manager, assistant director of nursing, and assistant administrator. She worked part-time as a nurse to pursue others dreams, hopes, and goals that she wanted to do in her life—as a volunteer disaster nurse for various well-known organizations from hurricanes to power outages for the people. She was also an artist, writer, public speaker, and motivational speaker. She raised money with her art and writing for families affected by disasters as fires, health, the literacy foundation, and people with disabilities. Many did not know all this within her circle or family.

She opened an art gallery (see newspaper story). After taking a financial plummet in a length of time, she had to close her gallery but was able to help young and inspiring artists display their work for others to see.

In fact, the article about my gallery was on the front page of the newspaper, and one day, when I went to work, there were a group of nurses at the nurses' station. They all paused when they saw me coming down the hall. One nurse stood up with an angry expression on her face and said, "I don't understand! If you can paint, draw, and write, why are you working here as a nurse?" I replied, "Because I love all three of these things, and I choose to do them and I choose to also work as a nurse too 'cause this is another one of the things I love to do."

Another nurse was so angry she was spreading rumors about me 'cause she was hatefully jealous and brought her husband in to work one day to beat me up. She had tricked me into thinking that the man she brought with her was a new nurse, and I thought nothing of it since he was wearing nurse's scrubs, and they did hire many nurses, both male and female. If it had not been for God's Holy Angels watching over me, I probably would not be writing this book. The man turned out to be her husband, who was just released from prison after shooting his neighbor. When I think back, I remember the man (her husband) having hate in his eyes while he stared at me at the nurses' station. This was reported to the director of nursing, and the female nurse was fired for this.

This story was authenticated by a nurse's assistant, who knew this and warned me who the man was. Frankly, this particular nurse should have lost her nursing license. Jealousy is hatred; they both go hand in hand. A person cannot have one without the other. It's sad to think that someone wanted to take my life over a newspaper article or, as the truth is, wanted to take someone's life for a gift that God has given someone. These are the times we are living in now, and unfortunately, I don't see some things getting better as long as there are people who fight against God's teaching and His love. There will always be hatred, jealousy, conflicts, and much more.

A friend once said to me, "I know you must be hurting and disappointed that you had to close your place of business, but you will be okay." My response was, "Oh, on the contrary, I am not disappointed and not sad about it. In fact, the only thing that beats a failure is a trier, and as long as a person tries, then they never lose. To lose is never to try what you may want to do or pursue and don't go for it.

The friend did not like my response and simply said, "Well, I would be sad, but maybe it hadn't hit you yet to be sad." Obviously, she didn't know me very well, but since her mind was made up that I would eventually be sad, I just let her go with that thought 'cause once a person mind is made up, who am I to try and explain myself to them? It would just be a waste of my time, and I do not like wasted time, but I love productive time. I was happy with my decision about closing shop and did not have to look down because I wanted it, I pursued it, and I did it. Even going out of business was my own decision 'cause I am for my comfortable decision.

New Business

Owners Darlene Jamison stand in the gallery of Art Designs and More, 3024 North Lindbergh Blvd., St. Ann. The unique enterprise plans to donate monies earned to area nursing homes for activities for the residents' aide, Jamison, a licensed practical nurse. She said the new gallery will carry her own designs in the style of Japan, China, and other cultures, featuring silhouettes. It also will display landscapes and floral arrangements. "I enjoy it, and it makes people happy," Jamison said about her art. The store is open from 11 a.m. to 7 p.m. Sunday, Monday, and Wednesday; and from 10 a.m. to 2 p.m. Tuesday and Thursday; and from 11 a.m. to 8 p.m. Friday and Saturday. For more information, call (314) 3443500.

About the Author

I was born into a life of poverty. I had to drop out of school at the age of fourteen to work in order to feed and clothe myself. I tried to be strong-minded and strong in my will to survive. Most importantly, I had to remain in my faith in God to be strong even as I grew into adulthood. I didn't get my high school diploma until I became an adult. Once I obtained my diploma, I attended two different colleges to educate myself. I became a nurse and was promoted after a year as a nurse administration. The administration saw something in me that I didn't see. They promoted me to assistant director of nursing and assistant nursing administrator. I was also an artist and opened up an art gallery and donated many pieces of my paintings to organizations to raise money for people with disabilities and for people in need. Eventually, I became a volunteer nurse for two well-known organizations to help others during disasters. I had two beautiful children who are now adults, and I am a grandmother of four. My drive to raise my children in a middle-class environment was important to me because I did not want them to grow up the way I had to. I wanted and gave a better life for my children. There was a lot of abuse in my life while growing up, and that was not going to happen to my children.

After a divorce, I met a man at work who seemed like the perfect gentleman. We dated for two years before we got married. That's when my nightmare began. Little did I know that he was the devil himself. I went through emotional, verbal, mental, and physical abuse; and I had to find a way out of his living hell. He was plotting on me since day one, and I unwittingly had no clue of this. No one should stay in any abusive relationship or marriage 'cause there is always a way out before he plan to murder you. But there is always a way out, and I found it. Learn from my life in order to help your life, and never give up on your hope, dreams, goals, and faith in the Lord. This is your guidance to peace.